Underwater [Friends]

By Lieba Gou[i]
Illustrated by Jane T[ ]

GW01003505

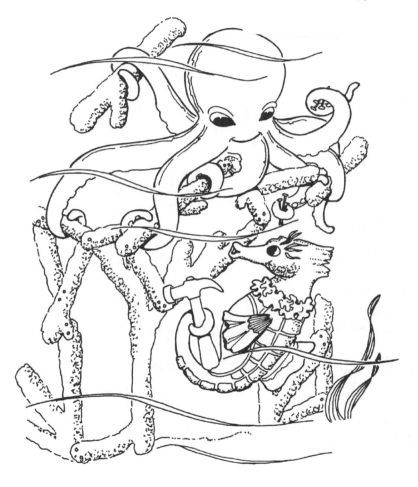

Common Sense Press
™

Common Sense Press
8786 Highway 21
Melrose, FL 32666
Website: http://www.commonsensepress.com

Printed in the United States of America
ISBN 1-880892-74-X

CONTENTS

A SURPRISE PARTY

It was a fine day in the reef.

Octopus and Seahorse were hanging a banner.

It said, "Happy Birthday, Tuna!"

"I can hardly wait to see Tuna's face when she comes in," said Seahorse.

"I love surprises!"

"And I can hardly wait to taste the cake," said Octopus.

"I love good things to eat.

Where is Lobster?

Tuna will be here soon."

"Should I call him?" asked Seahorse.

"Yes," said Octopus, "here is the phone. Tell him to hurry!"

Seahorse dialed Lobster's number.

"Hello?" answered Lobster. "Who is it?"

"Hi, Lobster. It's me, Seahorse."

"Hurry, Lobster!
The party is about to begin!"
said Seahorse.

"Oh," said Lobster,
"I did not tell you?
I am not coming.

I do not think surprise parties are fun.
Besides, Tuna will think it is a silly idea."

"Oh," Seahorse said sadly.

"Goodbye," said Lobster.

"Goodbye," said Seahorse.

Octopus saw the sad look on his friend's face.
"What is wrong?" he asked Seahorse.
"Is Lobster coming?"

"No," said Seahorse,
"Lobster does not like surprise parties.

He says Tuna will think it is a silly idea."

Now Octopus felt sad, too.

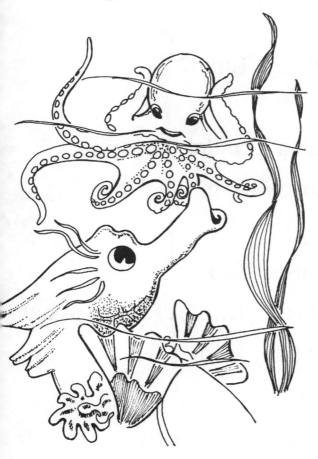

"What should
we do?
We have already
made the cake,
and Tuna is on
her way."

Seahorse shook
his head.
"Maybe it is
a silly idea."

Just then, Tuna swam in.

"Hi, friends," she said.

She read the banner.

It said, "Happy Birthday, Tuna!"

Tuna swirled around in a circle.

"Wow! A surprise party for me?"

Seahorse and Octopus smiled.

"You do not think it is a silly idea?" they asked.

Tuna smiled back at her friends.

"Not at all!" she said.

"I am happy to have a birthday party.

Thank you."

A NEW FRIEND

"Have you seen the new fish in the reef?"
Octopus asked Tuna.

Tuna laughed, "I sure have!
She looks funny!"

Octopus nodded his head.
"Yes, that is what I think," he said.
"I have never seen a fish like her before."

"I have an idea," said Tuna.
"Let's go see if we can find her."

Octopus and Tuna began swimming around the coral.

In and out.

Over and under.

It did not take long to find the new fish.

She was cleaning up an old part of the reef.

"Hi," she said.

"I am Clownfish.

Who are you?"

"Oh, hi," said Tuna.

"I am Tuna, and this is my friend, Octopus."

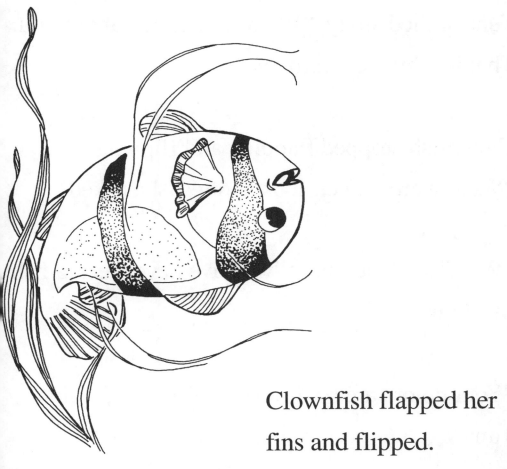

Clownfish flapped her
fins and flipped.
"I am so glad you swam over," she said.
"I could hardly wait to meet my new reef
friends."

Tuna smiled shyly, "We were curious about you.
That is why we swam over."

Clownfish stopped flapping and flipping.
"What were you curious about?" she asked.

"Well," said Octopus, "we have never seen a fish
like you."

"Your colors are so different from ours," said
Tuna.

"Yes, my colors are different.
 But look! We all look different.
That makes each of us special," said Clownfish.

Octopus and Tuna looked at each other.

Clownfish was right.

Everyone in the whole reef looked different.

That did not stop them from being friends.
In fact, that made being friends more fun!

"Clownfish," said Tuna,
"we are glad you have come to our reef."

Clownfish smiled.
"Thanks, it is great to be here."

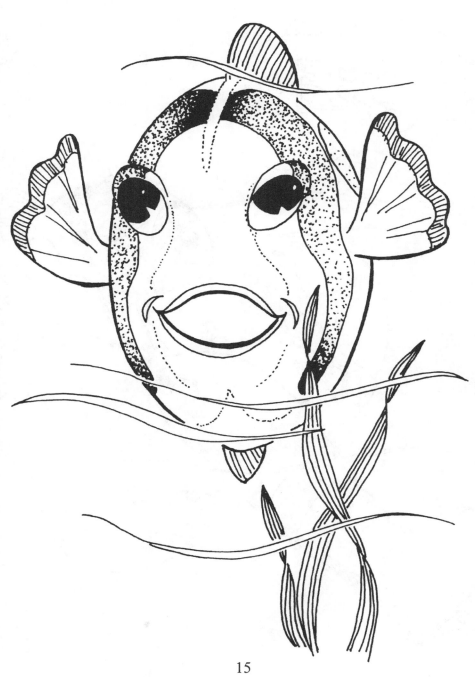

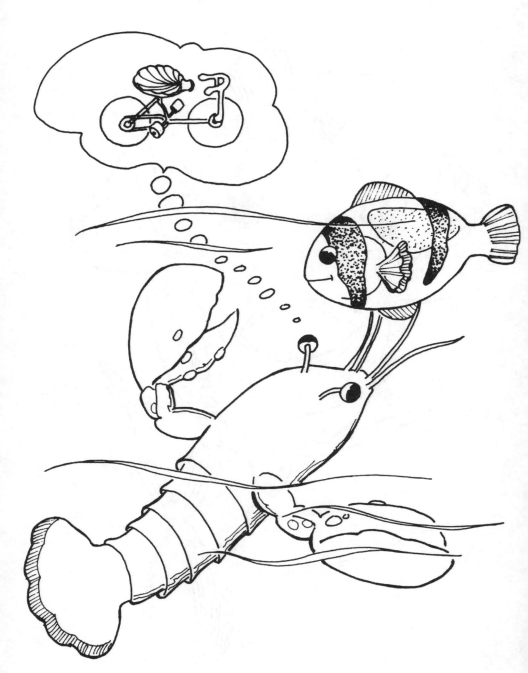

A NEW BIKE FOR LOBSTER

Lobster wanted a brand new aqua bike.
"My new bike will be the best in the reef!"
Lobster said to Clownfish.

"How will you pay for such a nice bike?" asked
Clownfish.

Lobster already had a plan.
"I am going to have a big yard sale.
I will make lots of money."

"I will help you," said Clownfish.

"I have some old things you may have to sell."

"Good," said Lobster, "bring them to me.

Today I will have my sale."

Clownfish swam home.

Quickly, she gathered some old things.

She put them in her bag and swam back.

Lobster had a table filled with things to sell.

"Clownfish," said Lobster, "do me a favor.

Make a sign that says,

'BIG SALE! PLEASE COME!'"

"Sure!" said Clownfish.

Lobster was excited. "Clownfish, tomorrow I will have my new aqua bike!"

Soon, Seahorse swam by.

He looked at the things that were for sale.

He did not buy anything.

Next, Tuna swam by.

She looked at the things that were for sale.

She did not buy anything.

"Don't you need a new hat?

How about a sand dollar?"

Lobster asked Tuna.

"No, thanks," said Tuna.

"I want to save my money."

Everyone in the reef swam by.

No one wanted to buy anything.

"I thought I would get my new aqua bike
tomorrow," sighed Lobster.

Clownfish asked,

"How much money have you made?"

"I did not sell anything,

so I do not have any money.

Next time, I will make the money before I spend

it," said Lobster.

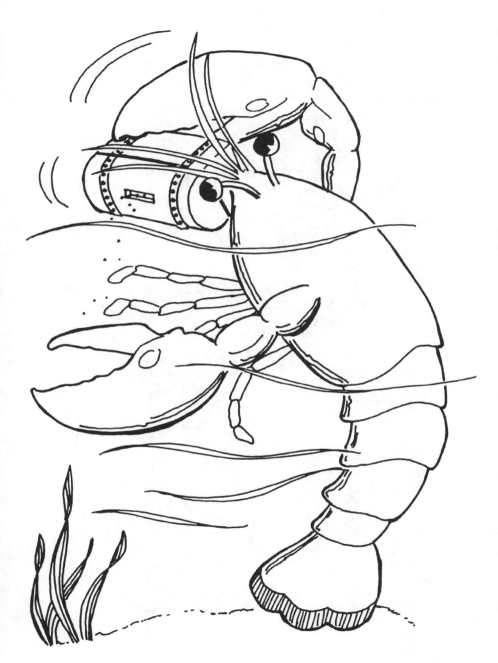

A BARN FOR SEAHORSE

Seahorse was happy.

Today he would begin to build his coral barn.

He could picture it in his mind.

"I will find the best coral to build my barn,"

said Seahorse.

"It will be strong and beautiful!"

Soon he came to his favorite place in the reef.

The coral looked strong and beautiful!

He pulled out his hammer.

Then he reached into his pocket for nails.

Carefully, he began to build the doorway.

He could not hold the door and hammer the nails at the same time.

"That is O.K.," he said.
"I will work on the roof instead."
He reached into his pocket for more nails.
Very carefully, he began to build the roof.
He could not hold the roof and hammer the nails at the same time.
Seahorse began to feel sad.

"What should I do?"
Seahorse asked himself.
"I really want to build my barn today."

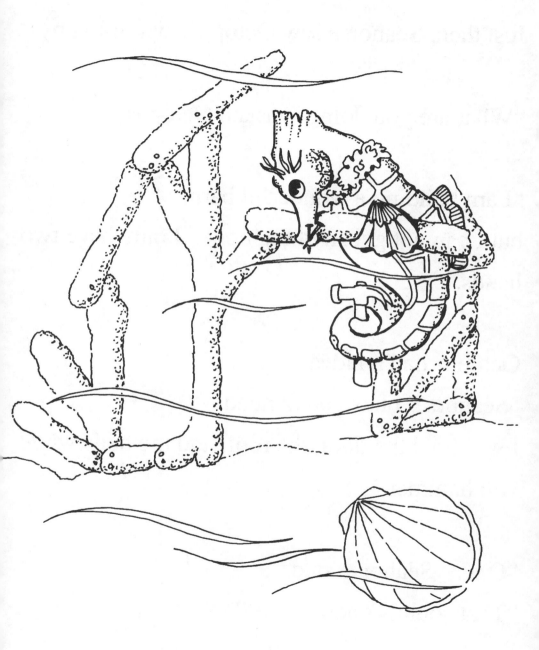

Just then, Seahorse saw Octopus swimming by.

"What are you doing?" asked Octopus.

"I am building a wonderful barn,
but I can not get anything done. I only have two
hands."

Octopus had an idea.
"Seahorse, I have eight hands.
I will hold the door, the roof, and the nails while
you hammer."

"O.K.," Seahorse said.
"That sounds good to me!"

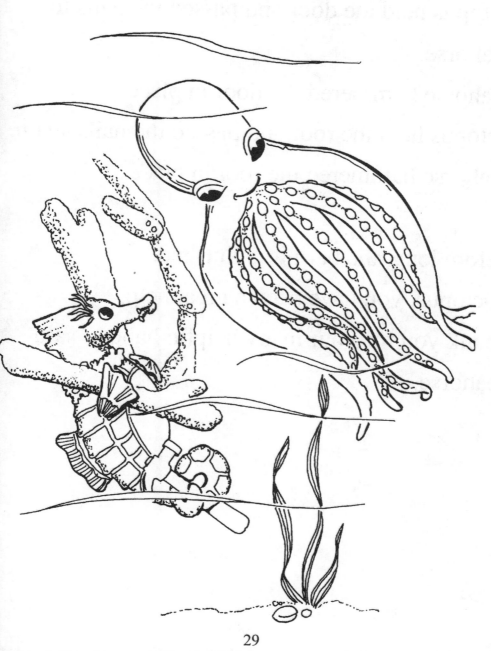

Octopus held the door and passed the nails to Seahorse.

Seahorse hammered the door in place.

Octopus held the roof and passed the nails again.

Seahorse hammered the roof in place.

Before long, the barn was finished.

"Octopus, you have been a great help.

Thank you for your many helpful hands," said Seahorse.

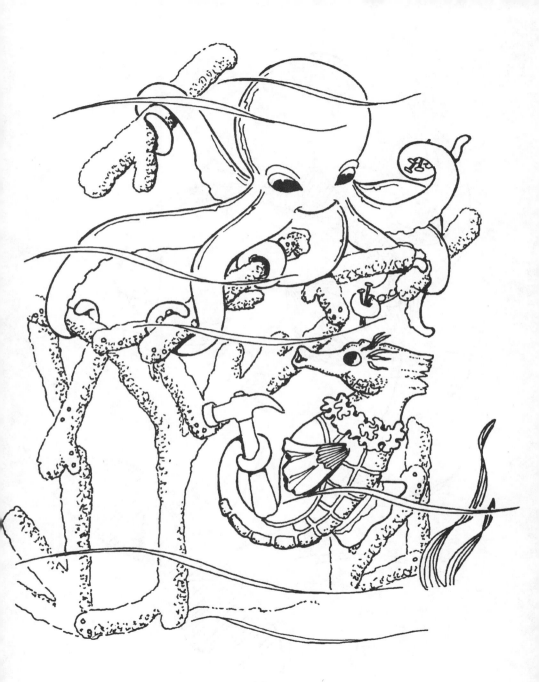

KEEP IT UP

Tuna wanted to learn how to juggle.
She had been trying for eight days.

"Maybe Octopus could help me," thought Tuna.
She swam over to her friend's coral home.

"Octopus," said Tuna, "I am trying to learn how
to juggle.
Do you have any tips?"

"Hmm," said Octopus, "try swimming in a
straight line."

Tuna sighed,
"I have already done that."

"Oh well," said Octopus,
"I don't know what else to tell you.
Maybe Seahorse could help you."

So Tuna swam over to Seahorse's coral barn.
On her way, she tried to swim straighter.
It did not help.

"Seahorse," said Tuna,
"I am trying to learn how to juggle.
Do you have any tips?"

Hmm," said Seahorse, "try starting with only

two shells.

Maybe that would be easier than three."

Tuna sighed, "I have already done that."

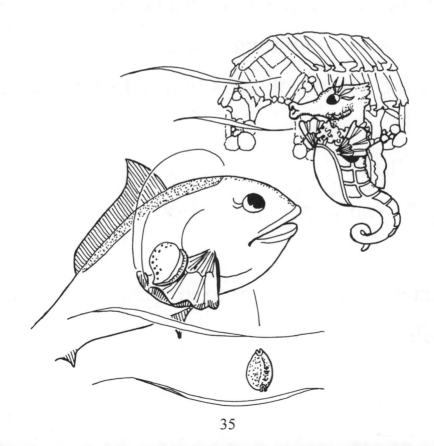

"Oh well," said Seahorse,

"I don't know what else to tell you.

Maybe Lobster could help."

Tuna swam over to Lobster's house.

On her way, she tried using two shells.

It did not help. She still could not juggle.

Her fins were beginning to ache!

When she got to Lobster's house, he was busy.

"Hello, Tuna.

What do you want?" asked Lobster.

"Lobster, I want to learn to juggle," said Tuna.

 "Could you help me?"

obster put down

is book.

Well, it's been a

ong time since I've

uggled.

But I guess I

ould help you.

how me what you

lready know."

una began tossing her shells.

She remembered the tips from her friends.

She tried her best to juggle.

This time she did not drop them as quickly.

"Tuna," said Lobster, "it looks like you are doing just fine.

Keep going. You have almost got it!"

Again, Tuna tossed her shells.

This time she did not drop the shells at all!

"I did it, Lobster! I did it!" shouted Tuna.

"Of course you did.

You kept trying and did not give up," said Lobster